365
Ways to
HELP YOUR
CHILD LEARN
& ACHIEVE

CHERI FULLER

PIÑON PRESS

P.O. Box 35007, Colorado Springs, Colorado 80935

Library of Congress Catalog Card Number: 94-67029

ISBN 08910-98542

Cover illustration: Bob Fuller

Printed in the United States of America

Published in association with the literary agency of Alive Communications, P.O. Box 49068, Colorado Springs, CO 80949.

To Christopher Kenton Fuller

A Note to Parents

Since you have bought this book, it shows you have a great interest in helping your child succeed. Please accept a vote of confidence and a pat on the back from me— because your involvement is an important part of your child's learning. Research shows there is a crucial connection between parents' interest and involvement in kids' learning and their progress in school. But it's not always easy to know how to develop their curiosity or how to boost their appetite for learning.

I believe all parents want the best for their children and especially want to help them learn and succeed in school and life. But many of us moms and dads today are busy with jobs, household responsibilities, community and church duties, carpooling children to soccer, piano, hockey practice. Just to list some of them makes me feel tired! We're often going in fast forward with little time to spare.

This little book meets the needs of our

busy generation of parents. It's easy to read. It has lots of practical ideas that build skills in reading, writing, problem-solving, critical thinking, math and science, geography, history, and other important skills. Many of the activities are things I did with my children during their growing-up years. On any day of the year, you can pull an idea, use it, and see your child's motivation and interest in learning rise. You can gear the activities to your child's age and personal interests, and use them as a springboard for your own ideas and creativity.

These activities offer many immediate and long-term benefits for your child: They develop a positive attitude about learning, increase attention span and focus on tasks, improve self-esteem, develop creativity, heighten curiosity, promote initiative and a willingness to try, encourage new interests, develop organizational and study skills, improve memory, develop a sense of security and a stronger parent-child relationship.

Since much of children's learning takes place outside the classroom, it is vital for you to be aware of teachable moments and provide opportunities to learn not only at school, but also at home and "on the go." *365 Ways to Help Your Child Learn and Achieve* will help you do just that. Most of all, enjoy your children today and every day (they grow up so fast!). Happy learning!

1

When your child asks a question
you can't answer, such as "Why can't I see
the wind?" write it on an index card.
When you're by the library,
get a book on it or check with
the reference librarian to help you,
and discover the answer together.

2

With a can of refrigerator breadstick
dough, let your child form her name in big
letters on a cookie sheet. Brush with
melted butter or beaten egg, and bake
fifteen minutes at 350 degrees.

3

Send your child on a newspaper
scavenger hunt: Find and clip a baseball
statistic; a movie that starts at 5:30;
a picture of running or tennis shoes;
Marmaduke and Beetle Bailey;
and the hottest place in the U.S. today.

4

Make paper-bag puppets with buttons
for eyes and nose; yarn for hair;
feathers, sequins, buttons, scraps of fabric
for costume. Then put up a tension rod
in a doorframe, hang a curtain,
and let your kids perform puppet plays
in their "theater."

5

Get a star map
from a local planetarium
or science museum
and take a "Stargazing Walk."
Identify stars, planets,
and constellations. Figure out which
phase the moon is in,
and tell stories about how
the constellations got their names.

6

Help your child get organized
by providing him with a calendar of school
and special activities,
a bulletin board, an uncluttered desk
to do homework, and a "school stuff"
box by the door for storing backpack,
completed homework,
gym clothes, and notes to take back
to the teacher.

7

Write a Lunch Box Love Note to your child
that communicates encouragement,
such as: "Good luck on your math test,"
"Let's go to the Science Museum
Saturday," or "I love you!
Have a great day!"
Even pre-readers will try to decode
the message, or you can draw
pictures to convey it.

8

Get a big chalkboard or white (dry-erase)
chalkless board for your child to use
to practice spelling words
and math problems, or to teach the family
the information the night before a test.

9

When you travel, play a license plate game
to learn the states. Provide each child
with a U.S. map and have them color
in the states as they see corresponding
license plates. The player with
the most states colored in by the end
of the trip wins.

10

Let your child measure the ingredients
when you bake cookies.
She'll get great practice in weights,
measures, division, fractions, time—
and have fun eating the results.

11

Make a "Writing Center"
in your child's
room with paper to write stories,
markers to illustrate them,
thank-you notes, and envelopes,
so he can express appreciation
for birthday and other gifts.
Don't forget to add stamps,
construction paper, and stickers.

12

Hang a map of the world on the wall
so your child can find the countries
and states where news events take place.
Use colored tacks to mark these
"hot spots in the news"
and place small pictures where family,
friends, or pen pals live.

13

Involve your child in environmental
"earth saving" projects, such as planting
a tree in a nearby park or putting
her in charge of recycling efforts at home.

14

On birthdays, Christmas,
or other holidays, give your child
a gift certificate to a bookstore.
Then go together,
and assist your child in finding
a book in his interest.
You'll be building a home library.

15

Limit TV watching. When your child does
watch a program, talk about it together
afterward. Pose questions about
the content of the show, whether the
characters changed, and how your child
would end the story if she could change it.

16

Use math to solve real-life problems,
such as: How long does it take
to cook a pizza?
How much gas did
we use on our trip
to Grandma's this weekend?
How many days or months
until your birthday?

———◆———

17

Be sure your child gets
exercise every day,
by playing outdoors at the park,
biking, swimming, running, dancing,
taking a walk with you around the block,
throwing a ball after supper,
or playing Ping Pong.

18

Keep a puzzle on the coffee or game table
for your child to work on
(with you, a friend, or alone).
Whether fifty or 500 pieces,
puzzles are great conversation facilitators,
develop spatial abilities,
help young children match colors
and identify shapes, and are lots of fun.

19

Take your child to symphony concerts,
ballets, and musical theater performances
to enrich his life and stimulate his
interest in music.

20

Play "Mind Math" when you run errands
or wait at the dentist's office:
Start with an easy set of numbers
to calculate: 3 + 5 + 2 − 4. If your child
has tackled division, she can divide
the whole number by 3.

21

Play card games with your child,
and make cards available when his friends
come over. Card games build many skills
needed in math and science,
such as sequencing, problem-solving,
counting, categorizing, visual alertness,
and discrimination.

22

Tape poems on the refrigerator
and engage in "word play" like riddles
and tongue twisters with your child.

23

Get your child a magazine subscription
in her area of special interest.
There are magazines about baseball card
collecting, dolls, sports cars, or anything
else, and receiving and reading
the magazine each month will boost
your child's reading skills.

24

Create a "Reading Hideaway":
Cut the bottoms off large cardboard boxes
and connect them to each other
with heavy duct tape—to make a tunnel,
house, or fort, and especially a place
to curl up with a book.

25

Design "Sweet Sculptures":
Use toothpicks and gumdrops to make
creatures, structures, and characters.

26

Teach your child to play
"Tick-Tack-Toe"
and "Twenty Questions,"
which enhance basic math
and logical thinking skills.

27

Get out crayons and markers,
roll out wallpaper
(out-of-date rolls are cheap
at wallpaper stores;
some samples may be free),
and let kids create their own scenes
of dinosaurs, funny people,
and animals.

28

Let your child clip coupons
out of the Sunday newspaper
and estimate how much money
you'll save. When you go
to the grocery store,
let him find the discount items,
give the coupons to the checker,
and keep half the savings.

29

Engage in storytelling as a family.
Tell stories of your childhood,
school days, pranks,
and how you overcame problems.

30

Teach your child how to use a calculator.
Then call out a word problem and ask her
to solve it with the calculator,
such as, "A dress costs thirty dollars
and is put on sale for 25 percent less
than the original price.
How much will it cost?"

31

Get your child a Rubik's Cube.
It's an appropriate toy to play with in the
car or on "sick days" and builds math,
problem-solving, and logic skills.

32

Collecting stamps, coins,
and even baseball cards
stirs a child's interest in history,
and at the same time
builds categorizing and organizing skills.
He can use a divided shoebox or plastic
organizer to sort and store his collection.

———◆———

33

Have your child make a map of your
neighborhood and mark friends' homes,
landmarks, and North, South, East,
and West directions.

———◆———

34

Take your child to a "hands-on"
science museum.

35

Listening to and participating in music
activities actually raises a child's I.Q.
Let young children make and play
a simple rhythm instrument,
such as a plastic spice jar with rice
or beans inside for "maracas"
or sandpaper glued onto two blocks
of wood. Older children can learn
to play a recorder,
lap harp, or guitar. Turn on music,
and let the children
keep time to the beat and play along.

36

Talk about the meaning
of numbers in political polls,
business graphs, and magazine surveys.
Explain to your child
the difference between a random
sample and a biased sample.

37

Invite an international student
from a local college to share a meal
at your home. Encourage him to bring
pictures of his country, family,
and pets. Perhaps he would teach
you a greeting or song in his language.

38

At the beginning of a family trip,
have your child note the odometer
reading, and then have her keep track
of the distance at "check points"
along the way to see how many miles
you have traveled.

39

Play the board game "Monopoly," which
gives kids a basic concept of probability
and problem-solving. When a player is
on Boardwalk ask, "How likely are you
to land on Community Chest,
or to have to pay Luxury Tax?"

40

Get your child an inexpensive
magnifying glass to take along to the park,
on walks, or car trips.
He can examine the inside of flowers,
take a closer look at leaves,
tree bark, bugs, or many other
interesting objects.

41

Provide a soft, stuffed globe
as a throw pillow for your child's bed.
As she looks at it or leans on it, she can
learn where many countries are.

42

Take your child to the grocery store
and have him weigh the produce,
count the change,
and price the best buy in cereal.

43

Encourage lots of drawing
in the preschool and kindergarten years.
The best writers and readers are children
who had many opportunities to draw,
scribble, and create at home
when they were young.

44

Using acrylic-base paints,
let your child design her own T-shirt.
Cut sponges in funny shapes, dip in paint,
then press on shirt. For extra pizzazz,
glue on buttons, lace, or jewels.

45

Buy your child a notebook
or journal and encourage him
to write the highlight of every day in it.
He can also use it for art sketches,
stories, poems, and great ideas.

46

Help your child mix a cup of liquid
dishwashing soap and a teaspoonful
of glycerine. Then let her go wild, blowing
bubbles with a straw,
a six-pack plastic top, or a colander.

47

In a small paper bag, put blank paper,
a pencil, and index cards with titles
for stories that relate to your child's
interests. Have him pick a card,
write a story, and illustrate it.

48

Give your child reasons to read.
If she is an animal lover,
find nature stories;
a budding baseball fan, sports biographies;
a space fan, science fiction
and aeronautics books.

49

To increase your child's concentration
and attention skills, work on a fifteen-
or twenty-minute project together:
assemble a small puzzle,
color in a coloring book, or whip up
a microwave snack.
Focus on just the task at hand
until finished.

50

Give your child a flashlight
and allow fifteen extra minutes
"stay-up-late" time if he
is reading at bedtime.

51

Give your child a bag filled with ten
to twenty-five of the same household item
(toothpicks, popsicle sticks, spools, etc.)
and using only these,
encourage her to design something.

52

Fill a box with dress-up clothes,
costumes, props, old hats—whatever
treasures your attic holds.
Younger children and their friends
can spend hours pretending.

53

Help your child design a family tree.
Talk about your family roots and traditions.

54

To observe the life cycle of an insect,
look for eggs in trees. Detach one gently
and place in large-mouthed jar
with air holes punched in lid. Watch daily
until caterpillar emerges.
Feed with leaves from the same tree,
and continue to watch as the caterpillar
spins a cocoon and turns into a moth,
butterfly, or other insect.

55

Provide your child with a typewriter
or word processor and plenty of paper.

56

Gather up the neighbor kids
and go on an Outdoor
Scavenger Hunt in your nearest park.
Give each child a list of things to find,
such as a bird's nest, tree bark,
three different pine cones,
types of leaves and wildflowers.

57

Teach your child to use a compass.
Make a treasure map for him by writing
simple directions such as,
"Go south two steps, east five steps,
north ten big steps." At the end
of the trail, hide a "treasure,"
like a certificate good for an ice cream
cone or a fun activity.

58

Have your child look at a framed picture
on the wall for half a minute.
Then have her close her eyes
and tell you all the detail,
features, and colors she can remember.

59

Let your child be the navigator
on the next family car trip.
Give him a yellow highlighter to trace
the route you plan to follow.
He can circle cities where you plan to stop
to spend the night and put a big star
on your destination.

60

When you have your next garage sale,
let your child help you price items
to be sold, act as your "banker,"
and serve customers.

61

Surround your child with books,
magazines, and other reading materials.
Keep a basket of library books
by her bed, a basket
of magazines in the bathroom,
a few books in the car, and a basket
of books by the couch in the family room.

62

Let your child set up a cookie, lemonade,
or snack stand in the summer to get
some real practice handling money as he
decides how to price his product
and spend the profits.

63

Watch a National Geographic special
together on wildlife, Civil War history,
the environment, or space.
Then talk about what you learned.

64

Establish a regular study time each day
and provide your child
with a quiet "study zone"
that suits her style—kitchen table
or bedroom desk.
What matters is your child having
something to read or study
every day
and your showing interest in it.

65

Be a model for your child and let him
see you writing, editing, and starting over
on a letter or project.

66

Extend your conversation
with your child by asking, "Why?"
and "Why not?" occasionally.

67

Work a crossword puzzle with your child.

68

Play "Name That Tune."
The first player hums or whistles
the first measures of a familiar song,
and the other players try to guess what
it is. The winner gets to think
of and perform the next tune.

69

Play "Concentration" to develop your
child's visual memory skills. Shuffle a deck
of cards and turn them all face down
in rows on the table or floor. The first
player turns over two cards,
trying to make a match, then puts them
back face down. The play proceeds until
someone makes a match, which rewards
that person with another turn.
The player with the most matches
at the end of the game wins.

70

Be a cheerleader for your child.
Look for what she is doing right
and sincerely compliment it.
Look for the progress she's making
in school, and point it out.

71

Make rhymes and encourage your child
to make them too,
such as "Silly Billy saw his friend Willy,"
"Give me the keys, please,"
or "Roll down the blind,
so I can find the orange rind."

72

Look over classroom papers sent home,
graded tests, and other assignments,
and commend your child's efforts
to study and learn.

73

Read aloud to your child every day
and encourage him to read aloud to you.

74

Give your child a daily responsibility
to carry out.

75

Play chess with your child.

76

Play the "Synonym Game" to enrich
your child's vocabulary.
Write a word like "walk" on a card,
and then brainstorm, coming up with
as many substitutes for the word
as you can: skip, stroll, march, saunter,
swagger, hobble, shuffle, etc.
Then try another word.

77

Have an "Un-TV Week." Get out games,
do art projects, chat,
and have fun together.

78

Help your child become an "expert"
on a topic she is most interested in.
Make an Expert Box:
Cover a box of any size with contact paper
and inside put tasks on cards that your
child can do to learn more
about her special topic of interest.

79

Demonstrate math concepts
with hands-on, real objects.
For example, show fractions
by cutting a pie into eighths or peel
an orange to demonstrate fourths,
halves, thirds.

80

Make a Memory Tray
on which you place six objects,
such as a hairbrush, quarter, fork,
toy truck, candle, and dog bone.
Have your child look at them,
studying closely for forty-five
to sixty seconds. With the tray removed,
he closes his eyes and tries to "see"
the objects in his mind's eye
and name as many as he can.
Subtract or add an object and repeat
the game, or ask what is missing or new.
Increase the number of objects
up to twenty, depending on age.

81

Use colorful sticky notes to remind
your child of chores, homework,
and other tasks that need to be done.

82

Attend parent-teacher conferences
at school whenever they are called.

83

Put your child in charge
of a family calendar. On it she can keep
track of birthdays, school holidays, trips,
dentist appointments, piano lessons,
and other important dates.

84

Count out fifty dried beans
(large size such as pinto or great northern)
and with a felt-tip pen or marker,
print a letter of the alphabet on each bean.
Put these in a jar and ask your child
to draw out a bean and say a word
that begins with that letter.
Then have him pick out three or four
more beans and make up a sentence
by thinking of a word for each.

85

Share your expertise and talent
with the school your child attends.
Volunteer to help in the classroom
or make some other contribution
with your unique skills.

86

Plan a Family Game Night:
Select an evening each week or month
for one child to choose a board game
to play with other family members.
Make popcorn and enjoy playing
and learning.

87

Encourage all the family members
to bring interesting newspaper articles
to the dinner table
to share and discuss together.

88

Play happy music such as marching tunes
or other uplifting instrumentals
in the mornings to set
a positive tone for the day.

89

Play songs in various countries' native
languages and help your child listen
and identify the language.
This develops the auditory skills to learn
foreign language more readily.

90

Help your pre-reader
and early reader make labels for the toys
and objects in her room
and around your home
(bed, teddy bear, chair, etc.).
Print the word for each object
on a card and tape it
to the item.

91

Computer games build skills and speed.
On a home computer or computer
at the public library,
let your child practice math basics
with a game like "Master Blaster"
or "Addition Magician."

92

Suggest to your child to write a letter
to the author of his very favorite book.
Send it to the author in care
of the book's publisher.

93

Help your child set up a budget
with her weekly allowance. Figure out
how much it will cost to buy something
she wants and how much money she can
save each week. Then provide other ways
for her to earn that amount
by doing certain jobs.

94
Encourage your child to write down
a short description of a TV program
he has seen and enjoyed.

95
Buy packets of seeds
and let your child plant
a vegetable or flower garden,
learning science by growing things.
Either in a fertile area of the yard
or in a "barrel garden"
(half of a big wooden barrel filled
with potting soil and fertilizer),
she can grow potatoes,
marigolds, or anything that thrives
in your region.
Don't forget to let her water
and weed her garden, too.

96

Have your child write to International
Friendship League (Dept. A, 22
Batterymarch, Boston, MA 02109)
for a pen pal in another country.
Mark the country on your world map.
Save the stamps from the pen pal's letters.

97

Check out library books that stimulate
curiosity, such as *100 Hidden Questions:
Answers About Dangerous Animals,
Insects Do the Strangest Things*,
or *Experiments with Light*.

98

In the car while traveling tell
"Round-Robin Tales": One child begins
the story, the next family member adds
some new twist to the plot or a new
character, then the story line passes
to the next person to continue the action,
and so on.

99

Set information your child has to learn
for a test (such as all the countries
of Europe, or all the states
and capitals of the U.S.)
to music for more effective learning
and remembering.

100

Have your child cut up the parts
of his favorite comic strip,
then arrange them in the right order
and write the story of what is happening.

101

Get out family albums, marriage
certificates, or other documents.
Talk about family history with your child,
such as where the child's ancestors
came from, what their occupations were,
and stories that have been
passed down.

102

Have your child unload the dishwasher,
stack and put away dishes, and set the table
to learn classification skills.

———•———

103

Find an industry in your community
that conducts factory tours
and have a family field trip to learn
about what they manufacture,
how they process and ship products, etc.
Have your child take a notebook to write
answers to questions she asks.

———•———

104

Help your child break things down
into small components or steps and do
each step. If he needs to read a 150-page
book in two weeks, have him figure
the number of pages he should read each
day, or help him break down the steps
to complete the history project
and make a calendar of each day's task.

105

When you go shopping,
include a stop
by your local library.
Make a few new books
for your child to read a regular part
of the shopping list.

106

Encourage your child to write
a monthly family newsletter
and type it on a typewriter
or word processor.
By looking at the daily paper,
come up with "news sections."
She can interview each member
of the family and write up
the headlines and stories.
Current photos of family events
can be added.

107

One night each month serve food
from a different culture or country.
Have your child locate the country
on the globe or world map,
and after dinner, read together
about it in an encyclopedia.

108

When traveling or doing errands
in the car, play the "State Game":
The first player gives
a clue, such as "I am the state that has
frequent earthquakes," or "I am the state
where Yellowstone National Park
is located," and everyone guesses.
If needed, he gives another clue on the
state. Each player gets
to be a state during the game.

109

Show your child how to make
her numbers line up in the right columns
when she is adding, subtracting,
multiplying, or dividing,
to improve accuracy in math.

110

To build vocabulary,
write a "word of the day" on colored index
cards. As your child learns the words,
let him decorate or illustrate
the cards and put them in a "Word Box."

111

Have fun with kitchen science.
Let your child put yeast on a banana and see
firsthand the decomposition of food.
Let her grow radishes, herbs, or bean
sprouts. Experiment with mixing colored
water and oil in a jar.

112

Encourage your child to draw
his own original greeting cards
and write an appropriate
message or poem to give
to family members and friends
for special occasions.

113

When you are cooking, ask your child
questions to stimulate her thinking,
such as "Why does the bread rise?"
or "Why does the cake taste sweet?"

114

Have your younger child gain a new
audience for his reading aloud by enlisting
his favorite teddy bear or stuffed animal.
The story can even be tape-recorded
for you to hear later.

115

Together, collect the leaves from a large
tree nearby in each season,
and press the leaves in wax paper
with a warm iron to save.

116

Read a story or book to your child.
Then give her some basic props
(objects mentioned in the story)
and have her pantomime the story.

117

Have your child make postcards
to send to friends or grandparents who
live out of town or when you are
on vacation. He can illustrate his postcards
with special scenes or activities,
use stickers to decorate, and write a short
message. (The person receiving them can
save them for your scrapbook.)

118

Leave lots of written messages
and notes around your home.
They can include encouragement,
reminders about tasks to be done,
and information everyone needs to know.

119

Actively listen when your child talks,
responding to the questions
she brings up and asking questions
to clarify her meaning.

120

Set a good example
when it comes to TV watching and reading.
Let your child see you reading
for entertainment.

121

Encourage proper speech habits,
helping your child
to use the correct words and phrases
and to learn new ones.

122

Have regular times for members
of your family to eat, sleep, play,
work, and study.

123

Create a Family Bulletin Board for notes
of all kinds—"Don't forget to clean up
your room," or "Good luck
on your science test"—to post
a comic strip or motivational saying,
give encouragement,
and enhance your communication.

124

Teach your child to estimate so he can
see if the answers he has computed
for math problems are reasonable.
When shopping, let your child estimate
the cost of the items on your grocery list
by rounding each price and adding,
then deduct any coupon amounts.

125

Help your child make up a practice test
the night before with questions
from study sheets, textbook,
and class notes. To greatly reduce test
anxiety and provide an active way to study,
have her take the test and score it for her.

126

Read the papers your child writes
for school, talk about them,
and make a copy of the best ones to send
to a favorite relative.
File in a "Best Work" manila folder.

127

Take your child to visit with his new
teacher before school starts.
Take a flower from your garden and talk
about the year's activities.
You will relieve many "school jitters."

128

When your child brings home writing
done at school, point out something good
about the story—the descriptive words
used, the interesting twist at the end,
the handwriting.

129

Subscribe to a daily newspaper
and encourage your child to read it
by involving her in discussions
about current events.

130

Your attitude toward math
will affect your child's attitude
in the classroom. Show him
how problem-solving math relates
to many everyday activities,
and be positive about how much math
skills help in school and in life.

131

Have a "Creative Night"
by providing
the raw materials of crafts,
art supplies, or invention.
Together design and put together
a banner to hang,
make a board game, puppets,
or anything that
appeals to your kids.

132

Teach your child to handle bills
and make change.
Put nickels, dimes, pennies,
and quarters in cups
of a muffin pan.
Give her a quarter
and ask her to give you
that amount back in different coins.
Or give her a dollar bill
and have her make change.
Playing "store" with real money
is a good way to learn about it.

133

Growing and caring for plants
is a good science activity.
Give your child a plant for his room
and show him how often to water it,
how to fertilize it, how to place it
in the room for the best light, etc.

134

Give your child a mail-order catalog
and a pretend thirty dollars to spend.
Have her look through the catalog,
cut out pictures of her purchases,
add them up, and see how much money
she would have left.

135

Provide your younger child a pail
of water and paintbrush, and let him paint
letters, numbers, and figures on
the sidewalk, the patio, the house, etc.,
to build large muscle skills.

136

Display your child's artwork in a special
"Art Gallery" at home by putting
her most recent drawing in a frame
and hanging it on the wall.

137

Let your child see how plants draw water
and food up through their stems
and trunks by placing either a stalk
of celery or white flowers in a glass
of red food-colored water.

138

Praise your child for a job well done,
whether that is a clean bedroom,
bringing home a good grade on a test,
or finishing a science project on time.

139

Set aside fifteen or twenty minutes
each day to talk with your child
about his activities, school happenings,
and subjects he is learning.

140

Make sure your child has a nutritious
breakfast before school.
Avoid sugary foods because
they can cause hyperactivity,
restlessness, and lack of focus.

141

Turn everyday chores into learning
opportunities by doing them with your
child: sorting laundry builds classification
skills; picking up her room together can
help her with organization.

142

Be a "Homework Consultant"
for your child
by being available to help
when he's stuck on a math problem,
brainstorming for a story topic,
or answering questions,
but don't do the homework for him.

143

Encourage stamp-collecting
(a great way to learn history firsthand)
by saving stamps on letters
that arrive from a foreign country,
watching for special history stamps
available at the post office,
and providing a small album where your
child can save and label them.

144

Have your child memorize poetry
or Bible verses.

145

Let your child make an original book.
Older children enjoy writing
and "publishing," but even preschoolers
can dictate a story to you and then
illustrate it. Covers can be made
of contact-paper covered cardboard
or heavy construction paper,
and pages can be sewn or stapled.

146
Volunteer to help take your child's
class on a field trip.

147
After notifying the principal ahead
of time, observe your child's classroom
by sitting in a desk at the back
for an hour or two.
By observing, you'll see how the teacher
teaches, see what is expected,
and get ideas on how to help at home.

148
Next to your child's bed,
add a reading lamp and a basket of books
on her special interests.

149

Encourage your child to begin
studying for a spelling or other test
ahead of time to avoid cramming.

150

Plan a family outing to a working farm
or a history museum.

151

Encourage your child to be observant.
When he looks at a tree,
ask: Is the bark rough or smooth?
Are the leaves dull
or shiny, long or rounded?

152

Let your child see you working
on a task from start until finish
to get a sense of the process, time,
and effort it takes to do quality work:
building a shelf, painting a watercolor
picture, making a dried flower wreath,
or repairing an appliance.

153

Call your child's teacher early
when there is a problem, and discuss
ways to improve the situation,
rather than waiting for the teacher
to call you.

154

Have your child interview
a grandparent or relative who lived
through an interesting event in history.
She can tape-record the interview,
write it later into a "family
history" story, and illustrate it.

155

For mental "aerobics," play Scrabble
or Junior Scrabble with your child.

156

Give your child the opportunity to learn
a craft such as cross-stitch, knitting,
calligraphy, or woodworking.

157

Read encyclopedias with your child.
Look at the illustrations, stop on the ones
that interest your child, and read and
discuss the surrounding information.

158

Play games such
as Battleship or Pente
to build logical thinking
and strategy skills.

159
Reward your child's efforts
rather than just the results.

———◆———

160
Give your child a disposable camera
for picture-taking on your next trip.
After the photos are developed, let him
arrange them in a scrapbook and write
captions under each one.

———◆———

161
Provide your child with math puzzle books
for building problem-solving skills.

———◆———

162
If your child is mechanically inclined,
look for objects at garage sales
or thrift stores she could take apart
(and learn to put back together)—
toasters, clocks, or radios.

163

Encourage and cultivate a sense
of humor in your child and,
most important, in yourself.
Look for comics in the daily newspaper
that tickle your funny bone,
tell jokes, and see
a funny movie once in a while.

164

Help your child learn to deal
with mistakes without thinking the world
has come to an end.
Share how we all make mistakes,
that failures—big and small—are part
of the process of learning and growing.

165

Let your child help you solve real,
practical problems, such as planning costs
for a family vacation, fixing a leaky faucet,
or figuring out how far apart
to space bulbs in fall planting.

166

Make sure every member of the family—
even three- to five-year-olds—
gets his or her own library card
and uses it regularly.

167

Let your child see you being curious
about the world around you,
through investigating things that interest
or puzzle you, your wonder at the sunset
or snowfall, and your interest
in his questions.

168

Suggest that your child carry a notebook
on your next outing that lends itself
to keeping a log of description.
Encourage her to take notes describing
a nature walk, animals she sees at the zoo,
or artifacts at a museum.

169

Use concrete things in your home
to help your child learn math concepts:
Let him measure the walls of his bedroom
with a twelve-inch ruler, a yardstick,
and a long metal measuring tape to see
how many inches equals a yard, etc.

170

Onto yarn or cord, string some items
found on a nature walk—shells, acorns,
seed pods, or miniature pine cones—
to make a necklace or bracelet.
Paint them with acrylics for extra color.

171

Fold a long piece of paper into fourths
and have your child draw an illustration
for the beginning of a story,
two for the middle, and one for the end.
Let her share the story orally with you
before writing it down.

172

Suggest your child make lists
as a way of becoming more organized
and using writing skills. He can make
lists of his favorite songs, activities,
friends; lists of things to do after school
and other reminders.

173

Put a large seasonal picture on the wall
such as Frosty the Snowman for winter
or a beach scene for summer.
Then cover the picture with brown paper,
and every day cut a small section
out of the paper cover
to expose a portion of the picture.
Have your child guess
what the picture
underneath could be,
and keep doing this daily
until she guesses right.

174

Make an "Activity Center"
for your child on a desk or table.
Include playdough, a small rolling pin,
scissors, magazines to cut out pictures,
paper, a hole puncher,
stickers, scotch tape, markers, etc.

175

Listen to radio stations that offer a range
of different musical styles: classical,
folk, country, ethnic, etc.

176

Avoid using dinnertime to scold,
lecture, or hand out punishments.
Instead, create an atmosphere of sharing,
talk about what's happening at school
and what's coming up on the weekend,
the next family outing, or anything
new learned that day.

177

Stock your child's desk
or study area
with everything he will need—
dictionary, pencils,
extra notebook paper,
a few big pieces of poster paper
for projects, pens,
and a suitable lighting source.

178

Contact the teacher
either by note
or phone
if your child
has a special problem
on a homework
assignment.

179

Discuss with your child
how important accurate directions are.
Next, have your child write out directions
for making a peanut butter and jelly
sandwich. Then give her exactly what
she has written out
(for example, if she didn't write
that she needed bread, just give her
peanut butter and jelly;
if she didn't mention a knife,
she doesn't get a knife).
After making whatever the result is,
eating it is the next
and most fun step.

180

If your child hears a favorite song,
suggest he learn the words by writing
them down while you replay the song
on your tape player.

181

Spend a rainy or cold afternoon
making and playing with playdough.
Mix in a cup of flour, one-third cup salt,
a few drops of vegetable oil, and enough
water to make a kneadable dough.
Use food coloring to tint portions
of the dough. Make cows and birds;
use cookie cutters
and other household objects to create
interesting creatures and shapes.

182

Visit a garage sale with your child
and figure out how many things you could
buy for seven or ten dollars.

183

After a rain, collect water from a stream
or puddle. If you have a microscope
or magnifying glass, examine the water,
then draw the small microbes
and insects you see.

184

Love your child unconditionally,
not giving hugs and affirmation only
for performance, but offering them freely
"just because" you love her.

185

When your child is doing homework,
eliminate as many
distractions as possible:
turn off the TV and CD player,
clear off clutter from the table or desk.
You'll be helping your child
focus and concentrate.

186

Instead of doing your
child's math problems
or other homework,
explain to him how to do it
and he'll grow to be responsible
and learn more.

187

Let your child
make a "magical" painting,
first drawing with crayon
on a sheet of paper, and then washing
over it with thinned tempera
or acrylic paint.

188

Encourage your child to read a history
or science chapter in small chunks,
and then to discuss what she has just read
or ask herself the Who? What? When?
Where? Why? How? questions.

189

Suggest your child
start on the hardest subject first
when doing homework.

190

Provide a working alarm clock
for your child to be responsible for getting
up on time on school mornings—
a much better start
for his day than a nagging voice.

———◆———

191

Instead of asking your child,
"What did you do in school today?"
ask to see a drawing, ask what she enjoyed
the most or found the funniest event
of the day, or ask about a specific project
the class is working on.

———◆———

192

Encourage your child to put in
his main study effort at the time of day
he concentrates best: after supper,
first thing in the morning,
or after a snack and play.

193

Put completed homework
in the same place each night:
in a box on the kitchen counter, on a shelf
by the front door, etc.

194

Make sure your child gets enough sleep,
primarily on school nights
and especially the night before a test.
Lack of sleep leads
to poor performance and anxiety.

195

Have your child write a thank-you
note to someone who was helpful or kind
to her this week.

196

After reading a story to your child,
ask him to describe the main character.

197

Using a TV listing, have your child
classify programs as fiction or nonfiction.

198

While grocery shopping,
ask your child how much more one
package of food costs than another brand.

199

Have your child read a newspaper
article in today's paper, and then ask,
"What made this story newsworthy
enough for the front page?"

200

Help your child set study goals
by suggesting she do twenty math
problems before going out to ride bikes,
or ask her to study until she knows
fifteen spelling words.

201

Teach your child memory techniques,
such as the acrostic HOMES to remember
the Great Lakes: Huron, Ontario,
Michigan, Erie, and Superior.
You can learn these from books
at the library.

202

When you bake cookies or brownies,
let your child put two in a baggie,
tie with a ribbon, and take with a "Have
a Good Day!" note to the teacher.

203

Provide a timer for your child's study time.
Suggest he set the timer for twenty
minutes, do half his homework,
have a break, and then set it again
for twenty minutes to complete
the assignment.

204

Develop listening skills at home
that help your child be more attentive
in the classroom. Listen to your child,
giving eye contact when she talks,
and suggest she do the same when family
members are speaking.

205

Show your child the clustering technique
for organizing ideas
in a book chapter or story.
In the center circle write the main idea,
and fill in supporting details
around the core
like the spokes of a wheel.

206

Encourage your child to take risks,
and praise him when he tries
something new—whether or not
he succeeds.

207

Get a stamp pad and rubber stamps
of animals, balloons, dinosaurs, etc.,
and let your child design her own
stationery, birthday cards, and invitations.

208

Be genuinely interested in what your child
is studying. Instead of asking,
"Do you have homework today?" ask
"How did the electricity experiment
go in science class today?"

209

If your child writes a poem,
frame it and display on the wall.

210

Speak to your child in clear.
complete sentences.

211

On rainy days when boredom
sets in, let your child make a tent
by throwing a sheet over a card table.
Throw pillows on the floor
of the "tent," add a few books,
and include a lunchbox
with snacks for him.

212

Catch your child doing something
good or putting forth extra effort,
and celebrate it!

213

Help your early reader read words
around your home, in the grocery store,
or on the road, such as billboards,
road signs, cereal boxes, recipes,
newspaper headlines.

214

Let little mistakes
and imperfections go by without notice.
Young people who are extremely afraid
of making errors or failing can easily lose
motivation and creativity.

215

To help your child memorize
anything from algebra formulas to dates
in history to French vocabulary words,
show her how to set the information
to music for better recall.

216

Encourage your child's
openness to new experiences.
Cook a new food,
try an unusual restaurant,
or visit an art gallery.

217

Show your child how to catch spelling
errors in a story or assignment
he is proofreading
by reading words in reverse.

218

Have your child figure out problems
on the calculator, and first talk
through how you would find
the answer—"How many gallons
of orange juice do we buy
and drink in a year?"
"How many minutes until your birthday
or until the school year is over?"

219

Buy your child a scrapbook and have
her keep award ribbons from camp,
school field days, Scouting, photos
of friends, favorite family events, and trips,
writing below each page what is special.

220

If your child gets stuck on an assignment
or project, don't let the obstacle cause
him to quit. He can go on to another
problem, get help, and most of all,
persevere until finished.

221

Encourage your child to read
directions carefully before taking a test.
Use an old test at home
to review common
test directions, and suggest she ask
the teacher if after reading directions
something still isn't clear.

222

When your child has a composition
assignment to do, ask him to "rehearse"
or talk about the topic
with you before writing.

223

Drop a cloth,
take out the paint
and a giant piece of butcher paper,
and get creative together.
Use big brushes and also
sponges cut in interesting shapes,
a marker taped to the end of a stick,
even apple cores.

224

Take a class with your child
at a local community center or YMCA.
Whether it's a class in karate,
cooking, square dancing,
or ceramics,
your child will see you learning
something new,
and it's a great
relationship-builder.

225

Save the raw materials
of invention—odds and ends
of stuff that can be made
into something else.
Your child can glue,
staple, or masking tape
the odds and ends into sculptures,
invent a new product,
and use her creativity.

226

Write a thank-you note to your
child's teacher sometime during
the first weeks of school
to express appreciation
for something that boosted your child's
enjoyment of books or some extra help
he or she gave your child
in math or spelling.

227

Encourage your child to undertake
a project such as writing his own book,
creating an original computer program,
or doing a science project and display,
whether it relates to school or not.
Whatever his interest,
let him do creative work in that area.

228

Check the weather forecaster's
accuracy. Watch the weather news
each day and have your child draw
her prediction on a calendar
(picture codes for sunny,
rainy, cloudy, etc.). Later, mark what
the weather actually was.
After one month, compute the percentage
of correct predictions
by dividing the total number
of days by days right.

229

Find a qualified person
to evaluate your child if he seems to have
problems in reading
or memory, or he is trying hard
but making less than average grades
in school.

230

Get balloons of different sizes
and shapes. Blow them up and let your
child release them outside one at a time.
Retrieve them and talk about how long
each balloon stayed in the air,
how far it went, and why.

231

"Get physical": Bowl together, go roller
skating, or play at the park.

232

Take a walk in the rain,
splash through the puddles,
talk about what causes rain
and how lightning develops.

233

When report cards come home
and are lower than you expected,
instead of grounding or yelling,
ask your child what grades she would like
to bring up, and help her write down
specific ways to meet those goals.

234

Be patient and supportive when
your child is learning new skills or making
adjustments to a new school
or neighborhood environment.

235
When your child
is participating in music, sports,
drama, or other events,
make every effort to attend.

236
Share your hobbies with your child.

237
When your child starts a brand-new
school in a new city,
ask the principal or teacher
to provide a "buddy" to show him around
and help him find the cafeteria,
library, restroom, etc., during
the first few days.

238

Experience what it was like
to live in a different era
by taking an outing
to a living history museum
whenever you travel.
There are sites
where reenactments of battles occur,
where your child
can step back in time
and attend a colonial school
or see village workers at their crafts.

239

Check out documentaries
and movies of historical eras
such as the Civil War, World War I or II,
the sinking of the *Titanic*.
After you see the video,
talk about what
caused or preceded the event.

240

If your child misses
more than two
or three days of school,
ask that her teacher
(or teachers) list assignments
and send home textbooks
and other materials
with a friend
so she can start catching up
at home as soon as she feels
well enough.

241

Build on your child's strengths.
Ask him: "What do you
enjoy doing most of all?"
"What are areas you want to learn about?"
Find out what he does best
and develop that skill.

242

To study for a test, have your child
tape-record class notes or the text
material, put it in a portable tape player,
and walk around the block
or do an activity while
listening and reciting the material.

243

Encourage making collages, crocheting,
weaving, or sculpting in clay.
These hands-on activities engage
most children's attention
and help them build longer
concentration and focus.

244

Sprinkle bread crumbs or birdseed
in the patio or yard, watch the birds,
and if your child is interested, get a little
book that helps her identify types of birds.

245

Play checkers, Chinese checkers,
or Connect Four games with your child
to develop planning
and problem-solving skills.

246

Experiment with the wind,
using kites
and pinwheels.

247

After you have finished reading
a story to your child
(or he has read to you),
ask him to tell you the main idea
of the story,
or to summarize what happened
in a few sentences.

248

Make a "bug-catcher" out of a plastic
jar with a tight mesh top.
Let your child collect bugs
and worms on a warm day.

249

Read an interesting front-page news
story with your child and then make a grid
and write down *who*, *what*, *where*,
when, and *why* it's important.

250

Suggest your child start
a small business
by having a dog walking service,
car washing service,
animal cage cleaning service,
or yard watering business.

251

Use acrylic paints, sponges cut in shapes,
and paintbrushes to paint old T-shirts
and give them a new look.

252

Let your child help you plan
and put on a block party for the children
in your neighborhood. She can plan
the games, make invitations, learn menu
planning and hospitality.

253

Start a bug collection.
Your child can catch non-poisonous,
non-stinging insects, put them in a jar
with a cotton ball soaked in alcohol
to preserve. Later glue them to a piece
of cardboard, label what kind of insect
each is, and look it up in an encyclopedia
for more information.

254

Save small plastic containers,
fill them with potting soil,
and let your child plant herb seeds
to make
a window herb garden.

255

Make up a batch of instant pudding,
spread it on a cookie sheet,
and let the finger painting begin.
Clean up (licking fingers)
is just as much fun as creating.

256

Make nutritious cookies
with your child
and then deliver some
to an elderly neighbor.

257

Have your child write a letter
to his two favorite sports, television,
or movie stars. Look up the addresses
in *Who's Who* at the library,
or send it to the team or TV station
or production company that carries
the actor's show or latest movie.

258

Teach your child to juggle
(preferably outside), using three sturdy
oranges or three rolled-up pairs
of different colored socks to build
eye-hand coordination.

259

Have a family sing-along time.
Get out your old instrument,
brush it off, and accompany the singing,
or play a tape of old favorites
and sing along.

260

Set up a balance beam for your child
to walk on in the backyard grass.
Use two concrete blocks
on each end and a long
two-by-four block of wood.

261

Have your child brainstorm
and make as long a list as possible
of twenty-five or more uses
for . . . toothpicks, leftover mashed
potatoes, plastic containers.

262

Give your child a collection of fat,
fuzzy, bright-colored pipe cleaners.
She can mold and shape the pipe cleaners
to make animals, people, shapes,
or anything her imagination dreams up.

263

When going on a trip to a new location, stop by the library and get a book about the state or city, such as *Make Way for Ducklings* (Boston), *Across Five Aprils* (Gettysburg), or *Now Miguel* (Mexico).

264

Throw a ball with your child after school or after dinner and watch the conversation open up.

265

Play the game "Simon Says" for practice in following directions. The leader starts, "Simon says—wiggle your ears" and the players do that. "Simon says—pat your tummy and jump up and down," and they do the same. Then he gives a command without saying "Simon Says," and the players aren't to do it. You're out if you follow a direction without "Simon Says."

266

Have a color hunt.
First everyone looks
for ten blue objects.
In the next round,
search for ten red objects;
then twelve green objects,
nine yellow items,
and four pink ones.

267

Suggest your child act out a favorite story.

268

Read a book of Japanese *haiku* poems
and then show your child how to write
this simple form of poetry:
The first line is five syllables;
the second line is seven syllables,
and the third is five.

269

Have a book party. Have each guest come
as his or her favorite character
from their all-time most beloved book,
and swap books with a friend.

270

Follow the election campaign
of a state, national, or local candidate.
Let your child collect the candidate's
information, find out his or her opinions
on the issues, and clip out newspaper
stories about that person. If your child feels
the candidate is worthy of support,
both of you could offer to volunteer
some time to help the campaign.

271

Take your child to the library,
introduce her to the librarian, and
encourage her to ask the librarian for help
in locating needed books and materials.

272

Encourage your child
to be on time to class,
open his notebook,
make eye contact with the teacher,
and stay tuned in
by asking or answering questions
and taking notes.

273

Each week, take the TV listings
and with your child circle the programs
she plans to watch that week.
Stick to the list and watch
only those programs!
If there's a special program
or movie one evening
the whole family
wants to watch together,
encourage her to get
homework done early.

274

A week before school starts,
set your child's alarm
for the time he will need
to get up for school,
and reset bedtime accordingly.
Then the first week of school
he'll be used to the new schedule
and more alert at school.

275

Encourage your child to write
down the phone number of at least one
or two classmates in each class so that
if she misses a class or gets stuck
on a homework assignment,
she has someone to call for help.

276

Teach your child how to be considerate
of other people who are using the library.

277

Instead of running up to school
to deliver a book or assignment
every time your child forgets,
let the natural consequences occur
at school so he will begin
to stop and ask,
"What do I need
to take to school today?
Do I have everything I need?"
before leaving.

278

Have everyone in the family pitch in
on Saturday mornings or on a designated
evening for forty-five minutes to an hour
of working together for house upkeep.
Write a list for each person
of specific things to do,
and when the work's all done,
go out for frozen yogurt
or play a game together.

279

Discourage the attachment of negative
labels to your child either at home
or school. Children become what parents
and teachers expect them to become.
Expect the best,
and use only positive labels!

280

Invite people who have interesting careers
to your home for dinner and include
your child in the conversation,
to help her begin thinking
about the future and her goals.

281

Keep a file of newspaper and magazine
pictures and photos. On a rainy day,
have your child select one
and write a story about a character
in the picture, or cut out a picture
and make a greeting card.

282

Encourage your child
to take a babysitting course
or first-aid and CPR course offered
by the Red Cross
or a community center.

283

Be alert for interests
in your child you could develop
to build talent
and self-esteem—things like art,
music, cooking, leadership,
pets, computers, etc.

284

Make your own family chore chart
or calendar to divide the work
and build a sense of teamwork
and responsibility.

285

Buy bright blue and gold construction
paper and ribbon to make family awards
for special effort, kindness,
or other positive character qualities.

286

Play with alliteration (a group of words
beginning with the same first letter
or sound) while you do errands
in the car with your child. Each
person gets a letter and thinks of a phrase
or sentence full of alliteration, such as,
"Pink pigs poked around pulling pears out
of pots and packing them in their snouts."

287

Think of five new positive statements
to encourage or compliment
your child this week that will build up
his confidence.

288

Start a savings account
for your child and encourage her
to deposit some of all money received
for special chores,
jobs outside the home or gifts,
and to record deposits
in a savings passbook.

289

Make sure your child
succeeds at something.

290

Provide colored paper
and an instruction book
on origami and let your child practice
paper-folding projects,
at the same time
developing his spatial and visual skills.

291

Avoid bribes, threats, and other negative
statements about your child's school
performance, which only cause
her to shut down more
about school and homework.

292

Be an active listener when your child
shares happenings from his school day,
tells stories he has made up,
or relates thoughts and feelings,
and he will grow in confidence concerning
communication and language skills.

293

Practice math skills with the active,
mover child by counting while jumping
rope, clapping, bouncing a basketball,
or jumping on a rebounder.

294

At the beginning of the school year,
preview each of the new textbooks
with your child. Help her get a big picture
of the topics to be covered,
talk about the parts that
look interesting to her,
and then you can look for videos or books
to supplement what's being presented
in the classroom.

295

On big butcher paper help your child
make a timeline of history dates
and events,
or classifications of animals
or plants being studied in science
to put around the walls of his room.
He can illustrate each event
or object on the timeline
and will better understand
the relationships between them.

296

Help your child notice
and appreciate the rhythms
all around us in everyday life: falling rain
on the roof, bells ringing,
the tick of a clock, her feet as she hops,
skips, or marches.
There is an important connection
between rhythm and reading.
Encourage your child
to clap or move to the beat when
playing music at home.

297

Give your child
the gift of your attention
and direct eye contact
when he is trying to ask you something
or express an idea.

298

For increasing auditory memory,
whisper a short message
in your child's ear,
and then ask her to repeat it.
Say four letters,
and ask your child to repeat them
forward and then backward;
then add two more letters and try again.

299

Put out some clay on wax paper
or vinyl cloth, along with straws, balloons,
Q-tips, and other interesting things
from your kitchen drawers. Let your child
make free-form creatures, favorite animals,
or other sculptures.

300

Provide Erector sets, Lego blocks,
and Lincoln logs for building to develop
spatial and fine motor skills.

301

Check out a library book
that demonstrates
a math concept in a fun,
visual way, such as *Caps for Sale*,
The Tenth Good Thing About Barney,
or *Arthur's Funny Money*.

302

Have your child find as many
triangle-shaped things in your home
as he can, and then have him find
round (rectangle, square)
things in the home.

303

Teach your child a song you learned
as a child. Then sing it together.

304

Have your child smell
each of your spices:
cinnamon, sage, ginger, vanilla, cumin,
and others until one
brings back a strong memory
of an event or happening.
Have her "talk" the story and then write
it down on paper and illustrate it.

305

Help your child grow a sweet potato vine
in a jar of water. Set it in a window
so that it will get enough light.

306

Give your child photos of grandparents,
aunts, uncles, cousins, and best friends,
a small album, and let him make
a "Special Friends and Family Album."

307

When your family takes a trip,
let your child make an ABC book about
the city or state you visit and its special
features. You can provide the information
for each letter and have her
illustrate each item.

308

Listen to a classical piece of music
with your child and try to identify
different instruments.

309

Have an "SSR" time after dinner
one night a week. "SSR" stands for "Silent,
Sustained Reading," when each family
member has something (magazine, book,
newspaper, etc.) to read, and a specified
time is set aside for quiet reading.

310

Visit the local newspaper office or library
and ask to see back issues of newspapers
for your child to discover:
What were the major headlines
on the day he was born
and on the day he was six years old?

311

Read your child a story
and then ask her
to draw a cartoon
or comic strip of the action.

312

Help your child set realistic goals.
If your son is doing D work in math,
encourage him to aim for a C
instead of an A,
which might be out of his reach.

313

Encourage your child
to try something totally new—
an adventure like canoeing,
a new food,
a new type of book or hobby.

———◆———

314

Show a healthy,
calm attitude toward
your own mistakes.

———◆———

315

Have your child help you
list five ways
to save electricity in your home.
Decide together which one
to implement first.

316

Set up a weather station
with an outdoor thermometer
and a handmade rain gauge
(set a fourteen-ounce juice can
in the open,
but keep it from blowing away).
Your child can take a reading
of temperature and rainfall
at the same time, morning
and evening, every day.

———◆———

317

Make a window feeder for birds.
Use waterproof plywood or wide one-inch
wood. Nail a lip all around the wood
to hold in the food.
Cut two braces to hold up the outer edge,
and screw braces to tray and house.
Your local lumber store
can provide detailed, printed instructions.

318

Visit an art gallery or art museum
together. Have each person pick his or her
very favorite piece of art
and explain why it is
to the rest of the group.

319

Have your child keep a record
of how she spends money for two weeks
or a month. On paper, she can list three
columns: Date, How I spent,
and How much I spent.

320

Have your child look through
the newspaper car ads and pretend he is
shopping for a car for the family.
Compare the price of several cars—size,
miles per gallon, safety features, etc.—
then pick the one
that is best, cut it out, and tell why.

321

Ask your child,
"What would happen if . . . ?"
and then brainstorm
about possibilities:
". . . you could go back in time?"
". . . it stayed dark all week
and the sun didn't come up?"
". . . everything turned red?"

322

Have your child
list your full day's diet
for a week
to see how much it contains
from different categories:
yellow and green vegetables,
citrus and other fruits,
whole grains,
protein, dairy.

323

Have your child
invent some new words,
define them,
and make up a "dictionary."

324

Play "Bingo" one evening
and have silly prizes
for completing a diagonal Bingo,
Blackout Bingo, Big X Bingo, etc.

325

Practice "pitch matching"
with your child as you go
about daily routines.
Sing to a specific tune:
"Do you want eggs for breakfast?"
and ask your child
to answer in the same melodic pattern.

326

Read aloud a high-action story
to your child
and ask her to try to picture
the characters
and action in her mind's eye
or on the "computer screen"
in her mind as you read along.

327

Try one of these ways to spend
one-on-one time with your child:
walk the dog together,
wash the car, fly a kite,
or visit a playground.

328

Buy a complete dictionary
and keep it on hand
to use whenever someone
asks what a word means.

329

Go over some guidelines for bike
or rollerblade safety, such as:
Obey all traffic signs and signals;
slow down and look
carefully before crossing intersections;
be alert for other vehicles; don't
shoot out of blind alleys and driveways;
give pedestrians the right-of-way.

330

Have your child memorize a poem
of his choice to be shared at the dinner table,
recited onto a blank tape,
or captured on video.

331

For math practice
and conversation-boosting time,
teach your child to play dominoes.

332

Help your child figure out how much
it costs for each person in your family
to eat one meal.
First have her jot down the cost
of each food used in the meal.
Divide the total cost
of the food
by the number of people
who will be eating the meal.
Then have her figure:
Is this more or less than the cost
of the group eating out?

333

Have your child write a letter
of encouragement to someone
in the hospital,
an injured pro athlete,
or a senator or congressman who has
served your state well.

334

Wash rather than discard
a Styrofoam meat tray
and ask your child:
What are some other things
we could do
with this Styrofoam tray?
Suggest he try one of the ideas.

335

Find an oxymoron on television,
in stories, or in advertising.
Explain to your child
that an oxymoron
is a figure of speech
in which two or more words are linked
but seem to contradict each other,
such as "wise fool,"
"new improved,"
"criminal justice,"
and keep a running list
on the family bulletin board.

336

Conduct a family spelling bee.

337

Doodle a few lines on paper
(straight or curved),
and then let your child
use her imagination to try to transform
the lines
into recognizable pictures.

338

Take a word or a phrase like
"United States of America"
and help your child
rearrange the letters to produce
as many entirely different words
as he can.

339

Play "I Pack My Bag"
to improve auditory memory skills:
the more players,
the more difficult the game.
The first player says,
"I packed my bag and in it I put a shoe";
the second player says, "I packed my bag
and put in a shoe and a pink rose";
continuing with each player
mentioning all the preceding articles
packed in exactly the right order,
and then adding a new article.
If a player forgets,
she drops out, and the game continues
until one player is left.

340

Take your child to see an artist work
at his or her craft,
whether the medium is clay,
jewelry-making, watercolor,
or T-shirt art.

341

Have your child invite three or more
friends over on a weekend. Get all
the ingredients for pizza: tomato sauce,
pepperoni, grated cheese, crust mix, etc.,
and let them make, bake, and eat
their own pizza creation.

342

To encourage language ability
and creativity, lie on the grass together
and look for shapes in the clouds. If a big,
fluffy white cloud reminds your
child of a sailing ship,
have him describe it.

343

Allow plenty of time for your child
to play because children learn a lot from
it. They need unstructured time
to daydream, make forts, or read.

344

Let your child know how important
an education is for her future
and specific ways education
or lack of it has impacted your life.

345

Encourage independence
by letting your preschooler
pick between three outfits to wear,
your preteen decide how
he will spend his allowance,
and your teen learn
how to manage a checkbook.

346

Eliminate negative,
critical, and hurtful
comments to your child,
and replace them
with encouraging words.

347

Make sure your child
has regular checkups
at the doctor and receives
excellent care for accidents and illnesses,
especially those involving
hearing and vision.

348

Make placemats so your child can
learn while eating.
Cut posterboard
in placemat size.
With bright markers,
draw around the edges—the alphabet,
math facts, the planets, etc.
Your child can illustrate.
Then cover with clear contact paper
so they can be
wiped off after each meal.

349

Take your child rock collecting
to a park or nature path nearby.
Find rocks of different colors and shapes.
Wash and polish them
when you get home.

350

Talk to your child about your values
and beliefs and your standards
for sexuality, drugs and alcohol,
and other important behavior.

351

Let your child grow a bean plant
with very low light,
and the same plant in a bright window.
Compare how the light affects
the growth of the plant.

352

Give your child an empty paper-towel
or toilet-paper tube
to take outside and get
an "up close" look at the grass,
the parts of a flower,
and other nature finds.

353

Write limericks together.
Find a book of funny limericks
at the library and read some aloud,
pointing out that the first,
second, and fifth lines have three strong
beats and the third
and fourth lines have two
(your child can clap the beat as you read
the limerick). Then suggest she follow
the rhyme scheme of the limericks
(lines 1, 2, and 5 rhyme;
lines 3 and 4 rhyme) and write her own
to illustrate and share.

354

Save magazines and let your child
cut out words that look
or sound interesting,
begin with a certain letter, or relate
to his interests or personality.
After finding and cutting out the words
in different shapes, he can arrange
them on a bright sheet of construction
paper to make a statement
or express a feeling.
When this "collage poem"
is finished,
it can be laminated by covering
with clear contact paper.

355

Figure out a special code
with the alphabet letters and numbers,
and then write coded messages
to your child to leave
on her bulletin board or inside
her school notebook.

356

Describe an animal with five clues,
and then ask your child
to guess the animal.
If he guesses right,
it is his turn to think
of an animal and give clues.

357

With your child find
an abandoned bird's nest.
Let her take it apart,
and talk about all the materials
the bird gathered to make it.

358

Observe what causes
your child stress
and help him learn to deal with it.

359

Play "Hide the Objects."
Hide six or more objects in a room,
in plain view, but camouflaged
or in a place that matches
in color to trick the hunters. Each player
gets a list of the objects
(penny, key, earring, paper clip,
stamp, button, etc.) and secretly crosses
them off and writes their location
as she finds them.
The player to spot the most objects wins.
Great for improving observation skills.

360

Know what math skills are to be mastered
at each grade level: for instance,
first and second, addition and subtraction;
third and fourth,
multiplication and division;
fourth and fifth, fractions, etc.
Make sure your child memorizes
all the basic math facts
and processes.

361

Help your child find out some history
about your community or town.
Talk to a senior citizen who has lived there
for a long time and discover where the
first school, church, and firehouse were.

362

Create and play a board game
with your family that involves
the use of make-believe money.

363

Find out a place of historical interest
in or near your city and go visit one
of them with your child.
Whether a monument,
battlefield, famous person's home, etc.,
you'll help history seem alive
and close at hand instead of far away
or in textbooks only.

364

Don't try to solve
all of your child's problems,
intervening whenever there's
a conflict at school or on the playground.
Let him learn from consequences,
handle his problems
whenever he can,
and he will grow in confidence.

365

Have high expectations of your child;
let her know
you expect the best that she has to give
in school, sports, or chores,
and remind her she can do it—
and achieve whatever
she's willing to work for.

Author

Cheri Fuller is an experienced educator who has taught at every level from elementary to college. She is the author of six previous books and numerous articles in *Family Circle*, *CHILD*, *Focus on the Family*, and others. She has also appeared on numerous television and radio programs, and is a popular speaker to parent groups and teacher seminars. She and her husband, Holmes, live in Oklahoma City with their three children.

Other books by Cheri Fuller, also available from Piñon Press: *Unlocking Your Child's Learning Potential*, *365 Ways to Build Your Child's Self-Esteem*, and *365 Ways to Develop Your Child's Values*.